D0538805

The Taxing Case of the Cows

A True Story About Suffrage

BY IRIS VAN RYNBACH AND PEGI DEITZ SHEA

ILLUSTRATED BY EMILY ARNOLD MCCULLY

Clarion Books

HOUGHTON MIFFLIN HARCOURT

BOSTON • NEW YORK • 2010

Thanks to the Historical Society of Glastonbury for all their help.

Clarion Books
215 Park Avenue South, New York, New York 10003
Text copyright © 2010 by Iris Van Rynbach and Pegi Deitz Shea
Illustrations copyright © 2010 by Emily Arnold McCully

The illustrations were executed in watercolor.
The text was set in Old Claude.

Clarion Books is an imprint of Houghton Mifflin Harcourt Publishing Company.

www.hmhbooks.com

Library of Congress Cataloging-in-Publication Data

Van Rynbach, Iris.
The taxing case of the cows : a true story about suffrage / by Iris Van Rynbach and Pegi Deitz Shea ;
illustrated by Emily Arnold McCully.
p. cm.
ISBN 978-0-547-23631-5
1. Women—Suffrage—Connecticut—History—19th century—Juvenile literature. 2. Taxation—Connecticut—History—19th century—Juvenile literature. I. Shea, Pegi Deitz.
II. McCully, Emily Arnold, ill. III. Title.

JK1911.C8V36 2010
324.6 2309746—dc22

2009034136

Manufactured in China

LEO 10 9 8 7 6 5 4 3 2 1

4500226394

With love for Michael, Cecily, Amelie, and Joe. —I.V.R.

To Alicia Suskin Ostriker, poet, mentor, friend. —P.D.S.

ABBY and Julia Smith ran their old family farm in Glastonbury, Connecticut. Feisty and independent, the sisters loved their animals, especially their Alderney cows, Lilly, Proxy, Whitey, Paisy, Jessie, Bessie, and Minnie.

5

For generations, the Smith family had helped Glastonbury grow. They had always paid their fair share of taxes, which funded schools, roads, and other services. In 1869, when the Smith sisters were in their seventies, the town leaders—all men—decided they needed more tax money. But they chose to collect an *unfair* share from single female landowners only.

At first, the sisters refused to pay. Abby argued that they should have the right
to vote on a decision that affected them. The town leaders ignored her. The tax
collector ordered the Smiths to pay a tax bill of two hundred dollars (about four
thousand dollars today) immediately. Frightened they would lose their farm,
Julia and Abby paid up. But the sisters, angered, began a public battle that
would last for years and would capture America's attention.

Taxation without representation—being forced to pay taxes they had no say about—is what drove the American colonies to rebel against England in 1776. Smith ancestors had actually fought in the American Revolution. Now, almost one hundred years later, men could vote, but women still could not. Abby called their own case "taxation without representation."

Throughout 1873, Abby attended town meetings and demanded the right to vote. Often the men would not let her speak. When they did, they ignored her, not even recording her appearance in the minutes of their meetings. So Abby gave her speeches outside—her stage, an ox cart on the town green.

When the tax came due in October, the sisters paid an installment of twenty-four dollars—12 percent interest on their yearly two-hundred-dollar tax bill. Male landowners were allowed to do this. But the town leaders insisted that the Smiths pay the total immediately.

On New Year's Day, 1874, a new tax collector, George Andrews, marched into the Smith barn. He demanded the seven cows, worth more than four hundred dollars, as payment for the overdue tax. The cows were to be held for one week on the property of the Smiths' neighbors, the Hales. If the sisters hadn't paid their entire tax by then, the town would auction off the cows and keep the money as payment.

The sisters—and the cows—were furious. The cows bellowed in protest as Mr. Hale led them away. "Nothing could exceed the trouble we had getting them into my yard," Mr. Hale said. "The cows resisted every way possible." He and his wife sided with the Smiths.

The seven cows spent the week in Hale's tobacco shed, which measured only fifteen by twelve feet. Crowded, the cows stomped and groaned. They needed milking, but they wouldn't let the Hales milk them. Abby and Julia had to hike over for the morning and evening chore.

Mrs. Hale wouldn't let a drop of the cows' milk enter her house. She told Julia that "it seemed the cows were stolen."

Demanding to vote, the Smiths stood firm and did not pay up.

A week later, Mr. Andrews led a rowdy parade down Main Street to the auction. Bessie, the best cow, plodded right behind him. The other six cows followed, prodded by barking dogs and a drummer boy. Julia and Abby came last in a horse-drawn wagon.

On the green, Julia recalled, "There were forty men waiting to buy an Alderney cow cheap."

When Mr. Andrews began the auction, no one bid more than a few dollars for the cows. Abby and Julia couldn't tell if the people were being stingy or being nice. Turns out, most of the townsfolk sided with the sisters.

Finally, Abby and Julia gave a male neighbor $101.39 to bid for four cows. Mr. Andrews flustered and grumbled, "Sold!" And since no one bid for the other three cows, he threw them in with the four.

Abby and Julia still hadn't paid their taxes. They had simply bought some cows for the amount they owed the tax collector.

Newspapers made heroines of Julia and Abby. Lucy Stone, a well-known activist for women's rights, penned a running account for *Woman's Journal,* the publication of the American Woman Suffrage Association. The *Boston Daily Advertiser* wrote: "Two Connecticut women are just now doing a mightier work on behalf of their sex than all the rest of the country." And the *Springfield Republican of Massachusetts* asked: "Is taxation without representation, which was wrong in Boston in 1774, right at Glastonbury in 1874?"

In spring 1874, the Smiths again refused to pay their taxes. At the town meeting in March, the men would still not let Abby speak. So again she climbed up on an ox cart on the green. She proclaimed, "Our town should act as a family, with people working together and taking care of each other rather than ruling over one another and denying the women a voice."

23

This time, as a penalty, Mr. Andrews filed legal papers giving the town temporary ownership of fifteen acres of the Smith meadowland. Julia and Abby, supported by neighbors, appeared at the auction several weeks later to buy back the land. But it had already been sold! Mr. Andrews had illegally accepted an early bid from Nelson Hardin, a neighbor to the north who had been trying to buy the Smith land for years. Hardin had bid only $78.35 for land valued at about $2,000.

The sisters vowed to get the land back. The tax law was clear: Movable property, such as furniture or working animals, should be sold before any land was taken for taxes. Abby and Julia sued the tax collector and Town of Glastonbury for trespassing and illegally taking their land.

In court, the sisters said they owned more than enough movable property to cover the tax bill. Mr. Andrews disagreed, claiming they had nothing of worth.

At first the judge ruled in the Smiths' favor. Then town officials appealed and won the land back. Finally, a judge ruled that Mr. Andrews could not take the land. He could, however, take movable property. And cows, obviously, could move.

Over the next few years, the Smiths still refused to pay taxes unless they could vote. They trudged back and forth to town meetings and to court. The cows tramped back and forth to auction. Each year, the sisters petitioned the Connecticut state legislature for the right to vote. Each year, they were denied.

During this whole time, several cows gave birth. The Smiths named some of the calves Taxey, Votey, and Martha Washington and Abigail Adams, after the brilliant wives of America's first and second presidents.

Supporters held fundraisers to pay for the Smiths' lawyers. One friend sold bouquets of cowslips, lilies, daisies, and hair from the cows' tails. The bouquets were tied with a black ribbon on which was written "Taxation without Representation."

The sisters eventually won their case on final appeal. They toured America, giving speeches and writing about women's rights until Abby's death in 1878. Julia died in 1886. Not until 1920 did the U.S. Congress add the Nineteenth Amendment to the Constitution, finally giving women the right to vote. The Smith sisters didn't live to see it, but they had played a part in making it happen . . . and so, of course, had their cows.

Authors' Note

Abby and Julia Smith and their three sisters learned activism from their family. At a time when most girls did not receive education, the Smiths' parents encouraged learning. Their mother, Hannah, could read and write in French, Latin, and Greek. She especially liked astronomy. Zephaniah, their father, had graduated from Yale University. He opened a general store and later became a lawyer. He represented Glastonbury in the state legislature. The girls themselves attended several different boarding schools, studied under private tutors, homeschooled, and lived for months "immersed" with families that spoke other languages.

Each of the five Smith girls developed unique talents and skills that few girls had in the 1800s. They became inventors, artists, musicians. Julia, a writer, had a gift for languages. The first woman ever to translate the Bible, Julia translated it twice from Greek, twice from Hebrew, and once from Latin. Abby grew up reciting ancient literature by Greek and Roman authors. These language skills served the sisters well in their suffrage battles.

The Smith family, very religious, held their own services and prayed together daily. They fought for abolition, holding antislavery meetings at home, teaching freed slaves how to read, and petitioning Congress. The family devoted its passion and energy to equality. Today, all of Glastonbury is very proud of them.

Selected Sources

The Historical Society of Glastonbury, Connecticut. Various records and publications, including the following:

Hedden, Daniel T. *The Glastonbury Express: A Photographic History of a New England Town over the Last Century,* 1990.

Housley, Kathleen. *The Letter Kills but the Spirit Gives Life: The Smith Abolitionists, Suffragists, Bible Translators,* 1993.

McNulty, Marjorie Grant. *From Settlement to Suburb,* 1996.

Smith, Julia E. *Abby Smith and Her Cows, With a Report of the Law Case Decided Contrary to Law.* Hartford, Conn.: American Publishing Company, 1877.

Ward, Geoffrey C., and Ken Burns. *Not for Ourselves Alone: The Story of Elizabeth Cady Stanton* New York: Alfred A. Knopf, 1999.